EXTREME MACHINES

THE WORLD'S TOUGHEST MACHINES

Judy Kentor Schmauss

Raintree

Chicago, Illinois

www.heinemannraintree.com
Visit our website to find out more information about Heinemann-Raintree books.

To order:
☎ Phone 888-454-2279
▨ Visit www.heinemannraintree.com to browse our catalog and order online.

Edited by Nancy Dickmann and Megan Cotugno
Designed by Jo Hinton-Malivoire
Picture research by Tracy Cummins
Production by Victoria Fitzgerald

Printed and bound in China by CTPS

14 13 12 11 10
10 9 8 7 6 5 4 3 2

Library of Congress Cataloging-in-Publication Data
Schmauss, Judy Kentor.
  The world's toughest machines / Judy Schmauss.
     p. cm. -- (Extreme machines)
  Includes bibliographical references and index.
  ISBN 978-1-4109-3878-7 (hc) -- ISBN 978-1-4109-3886-2 (pb) 1. Machinery--Juvenile literature. 2. Earthmoving machinery--Juvenile literature. 3. Industrial equipment--Juvenile literature. I. Title.
  TJ147.S36 2011
  629.04'6--dc22
                    2009051424

Acknowledgments
The author and publishers are grateful to the following for permission to reproduce copyright material: Alamy p. **4** (Tony DiZinno / TRANSTOCK); BAE Systems pp. **8, 9**; Corbis pp. **7** (© Transtock), **20** (© Juan Carlos Ulate/Reuters), **21** (© Duomo), **27** bottom (© Jim Reed), **21** top (© Gene Blevins/LA Daily News); DefenseImagery.com p. **18** (ROBERT K GYSGT BLANKENSHIP, USMC); Getty Images pp. **12** (SSPL), **13** (David McNew), **14** (CORTEZ/AFP), **15** (Car Culture), **19** (JEWEL SAMAD/AFP), **23** (Pierre Mion/National Geographic), **26** (Carsten Peter); istockphoto p. **5** (© Don Bayley); NASA p. **24** (JPL); NOAA Photo Library p. **22** (OAR/National Undersea Research Program (NURP)); Photo Researchers, Inc. p. **25** (Atlas Photo Bank); Shutterstock pp. **6** (Stephen Mcsweeny), **10** (Alexey Fateev), **11** (Frontpage); U.S. Marine Corps photo pp. **16** (Sgt. Jason W. Fudge), **17**.

Cover photograph of US 2nd Infantry Division M-1A1 Abraham tanks reproduced with permission of Getty Images (AFP).

Every effort has been made to contact copyright holders of any material reproduced in this book. Any omissions will be rectified in subsequent printings if notice is given to the publisher.

Some words are shown in bold, **like this**. You can find out what they mean by looking in the glossary.

Contents

Tough Machines

There are many kinds of machines. Some of them need tender, loving care. Their drivers keep them inside so they don't get scratched. Other machines are tougher than that. They do some of the world's hardest jobs!

Nobody polishes this machine!

Move That Dirt!

If you need to move a lot of dirt, a **bulldozer** is the machine to use. Its curved blade easily pushes dirt, rocks, and anything else out of the way. A powerful engine keeps it moving forward.

blade

EXTREME FACT
Some bulldozers can weigh over 100 tons!

One Tough Vehicle

The Terrier is an armored military vehicle. It weighs about 30 tons! On the front of the Terrier is a huge bucket. This bucket is used to move obstacles that get in the way.

EXTREME FACT

The Terrier can be operated by remote control. It also has night vision!

Dig It!

Excavators do all types of jobs. Some use their buckets to dig up dirt. This one is knocking down a house! Excavators smash through wood, rocks, and whatever else gets in their way.

buckets

This excavator has many buckets to scoop up dirt more quickly.

Through the Earth

This fierce machine is used to dig tunnels. Known as a **mole**, its front end has big steel teeth built into it. The front end spins around and around. The steel teeth cut through the dirt and rocks. The dirt and rocks are carried out of the back by a **conveyor belt**.

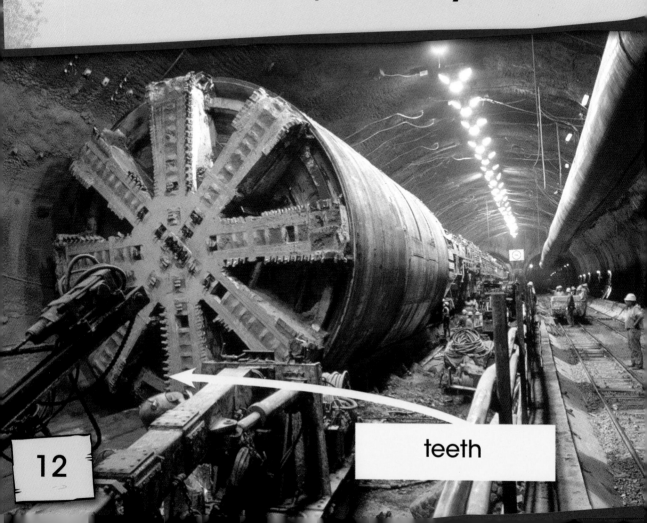

teeth

A Safe Ride

This is one tough car. Its tires can run even if they're flat. If a bullet hits the gas tank, it doesn't blow up. And the windows are bullet **resistant**. A bullet might scratch it, but it won't get through.

EXTREME FACT

What makes windows bullet resistant? A special material is put between two pieces of glass. The material helps **absorb**, or take in, a bullet's energy.

Mine-Resistant Trucks

In war zones, there are dangers everywhere. A tough machine is needed to keep you safe. This Cougar can take almost anything. A blast-proof body protects drivers from exploding mines in the ground.

A Mighty Tank

The armor on the M1A1 Abrams tank is so tough that rockets bounce right off of it. That's because the armor is made from a type of metal that is stronger than steel.

EXTREME FACT

This tank's guns can shoot a target more than a mile away!

It's a Monster!

Bigfoot. Gravedigger. These names sound like monsters. They are monsters all right—monster trucks! Monster trucks race each other over ramps and rows of cars. They crush anything that gets in their way.

Down in the Sea

Some tough machines go to extreme places. *Alvin*, a **submersible,** or underwater machine, takes scientists to the bottom of the ocean. The weight of the water would crush other vehicles. But *Alvin* is made of **titanium**.

Alvin found the wreck of the RMS *Titanic*.

Alvin

RMS *Titanic*

Out in Space

Voyager 1 was sent into space in 1977. It explores our solar system. *Voyager 1* can stand up to **solar winds** that blow up to 2 million mph (3.2 million km/h). *Voyager 1* might keep going for another 20 to 30 years!

EXTREME FACT
A disk on board holds greetings to aliens in 55 different languages!

Into the Tornado

This machine rides right into tornadoes.
It is covered with armor like a tank.
The armor keeps it from blowing away.
But this machine is faster than a tank.
It can catch up with a tornado—and
take pictures from inside it!

tornado

This machine needs to be faster and tougher than a tornado!

Test Yourself!

Try to match up each question with the correct answer.

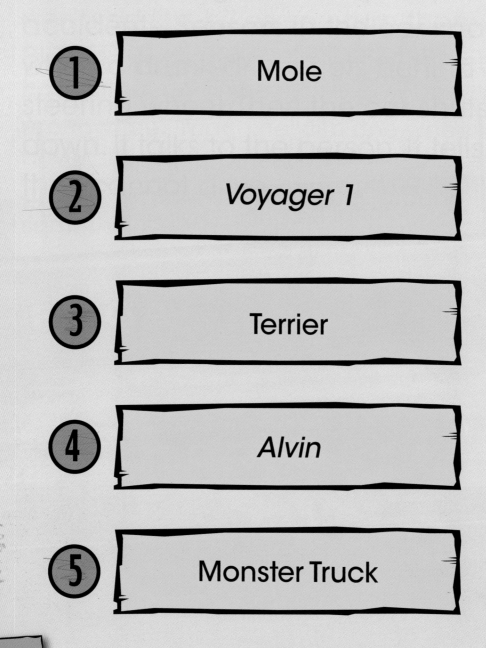

1. Mole

2. *Voyager 1*

3. Terrier

4. *Alvin*

5. Monster Truck

a Which tough vehicle has night vision?

b Which machine tells us about what's out in space?

c Which machine goes over rows of cars?

d Which machine takes scientists to the bottom of the ocean floor?

e Which machine digs tunnels?

Glossary

absorb to soak up like a sponge soaks up water

bulldozer a large truck used for pushing things

conveyor belt a moving surface that carries things along

mole a machine that digs holes

resistant to hold up without breaking against the force or effect of something

submersible a vehicle that can go below the surface of the water

solar winds winds in space caused by the Sun

titanium a strong metal

Find Out More

Books

Jennings, Terry. *Construction Vehicles.*
Philadelphia, PA: Saunders Book
Company, 2009.

Morganelli, Adrianna. *Trucks: Pickups to Big Rigs.* New
York: Crabtree Publishing Company, 2007.

Simons, Lisa M. Bolt. *The Kid's Guide to Military Vehicles.*
Mankato, MN: Capstone Press, 2009.

Websites

Everything About Construction Equipment
http://www.kenkenkikki.jp/special/e_index.html
Find out how bulldozers and other machines work.

Monster Trucks
http://www.monstertrucks.net/
This Site answers many questions frequently asked about
monster trucks.

Voyager 1 and *2*
**www.worsleyschool.net/science/files/extreme/
machines.html**
Follow the travels of *Voyager 1* and *2* through the
solar system.

Find out

How big can a
bulldozer get?

Index